How to Create Language Experts With
Literary Terms

Codi Hrouda and Emma McInerney
with Lyle Lee Jenkins

My Book of Words in the Same Family

By: _____

School: _____

Teacher: _____

Date: _____

My Book of Predictions

By: _____

School: _____

Teacher: _____

Date: _____

My Book of Main Characters and Settings

By: _____

School: _____

Teacher: _____

Date: _____

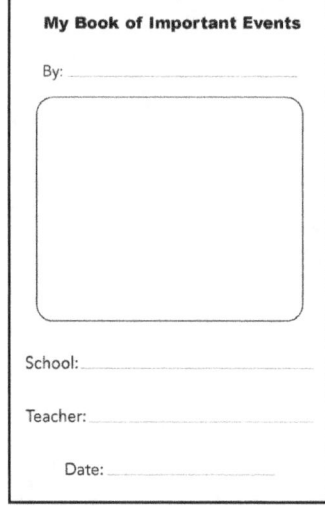

My Book of Important Events

By: _____

School: _____

Teacher: _____

Date: _____

My Book of Characters That are the Same and Different

By: _____

School: _____

Teacher: _____

Date: _____

Perfect School Collection™

To contact the authors regarding keynotes, workshops or bulk orders, visit LtoJ.net/Contact

ISBN: 978-1-956457-66-7

Book Design & Graphics: Christy Courtright, Christy's Customs LLC
Quality Assurance Manager: Kelly Lippert
Publishing Consultant: Martha Bullen, Bullen Publishing Services
Distribution Coordinator: Maggie McLaughlin

Printed in the United States of America

The Perfect School Collection™

How to Create a Perfect School by Lyle Lee Jenkins

How to Create a Perfect Home School by Lyle Lee Jenkins and Kelly Hawkinson Lippert

Perfect School Collection™ Resources

How to Create Math Experts series by Peggy McLean and Lyle Lee Jenkins

How to Create Math Experts with Fluency Quizzes by Peggy McLean and Lyle Lee Jenkins

How to Create Math Experts with Math Standards Quizzes by Peggy McLean, Laura Hayes and Lyle Lee Jenkins

How to Create a Math Foundation for Future Math Experts by Lyle Lee Jenkins

How to Create Bible Experts: Genesis to Revelation by Richard Douglas Junior Jenkins with Lyle Lee Jenkins

Early Readers

Bible Patterns for Young Readers series by Lyle Lee Jenkins

Aesop Patterns for Young Readers series by Lyle Lee Jenkins

Young Authors

Wordless Books for Young Authors series by Jim Chansler and Lyle Lee Jenkins

Special Project

All About Henry: Rich Widower of Savannah Valley by Lyle Lee Jenkins

CONTENTS

INTRODUCTION

The philosophy behind these booklets is that they are student-led, and elementary (K - 6) standards driven. In other words, students can independently complete much of the materials they are expected to learn in school with occasional pre-teaching.

The booklets are designed with a left-brain/right-brain balance. The back cover is a right-brain activity and the inside pages are clearly left-brain. The page prior to each grade level gives parents and teachers background knowledge and suggestions to successfully support their students and children through the booklets.

In order to create and assemble the booklets, parents and teachers can scan the QR code provided at the end of the book to download digital copies. To ensure proper printing, please utilize double sided printing and set your printer to "flip" on the short edge. The front page will be the front and back cover of the booklet. We have also included some bonus booklets within this series to support additional literary term exploration.

Enjoy,

Codi Hrouda, Emma McInerney and Lyle Lee Jenkins

GRADE 1
BOOKLET DIRECTIONS

Depending on your student or child's' reading ability, directions may need to be read to them.

My Book of Favorite Sight Words:
Students may need to be pre-taught what sight words are and given examples of sight words.

My Book of Words in the Same Family:
Within the booklet, the term "word family" is used. This means words that can be categorized together.

My Book of Main Character and Setting:
Students will need to have access to their favorite picture books and coloring supplies.

My Book of Important Events in the Story:
Students will need to have access to their favorite picture books and coloring supplies.

My Book of Connections:
Students will need to have access to their favorite fiction and nonfiction book.

My Book of Characters That are the Same and Different:
Students will need to have access to two fiction books.

My Book of _____ Facts:
Students are to chose the topic they would like to investigate and fill the topic into the title. Access to non-fiction books will be needed for this booklet.

My Book of Predictions:
Students will need to have access to a nonfiction book and coloring supplies.

Write a story using as many sight words as you can

My Book of Favorite Sight Words

By: _____

School: _____

Teacher: _____

Date: _____

Sight words - Words that cannot be sounded out so you need to know them by sight.

Read and sound out all the words below.
Circle the sight words:

Read a book and find as many sight words as you can. List them below without writing them more than once.

From   All   Them

Toss   Been   Did

Who   Does   Skip

The   Coat   Shout

List two holidays you celebrate and write their word families. Circle any words that could fit under either holiday.

Holiday 1: _____   Holiday 2: _____

_____   _____

_____   _____

_____   _____

_____   _____

_____   _____

My Book of Words in the Same Family

By: _____

School: _____

Teacher: _____

Date: _____

List words that have something in common with your word on the front creating a word family. (Ex. Books - pages, shelf, cover)

_____   _____

_____   _____

_____   _____

_____   _____

_____   _____

_____   _____

Use the bold word to create a word family

Outerspace

_____   _____

_____   _____

Animals

_____   _____

_____   _____

Food

_____   _____

_____   _____

Student booklets are available via the QR code at the end of the book

Draw your own main character and setting

My Book of Main Characters and Settings

By: _____

School: _____

Teacher: _____

Date: _____

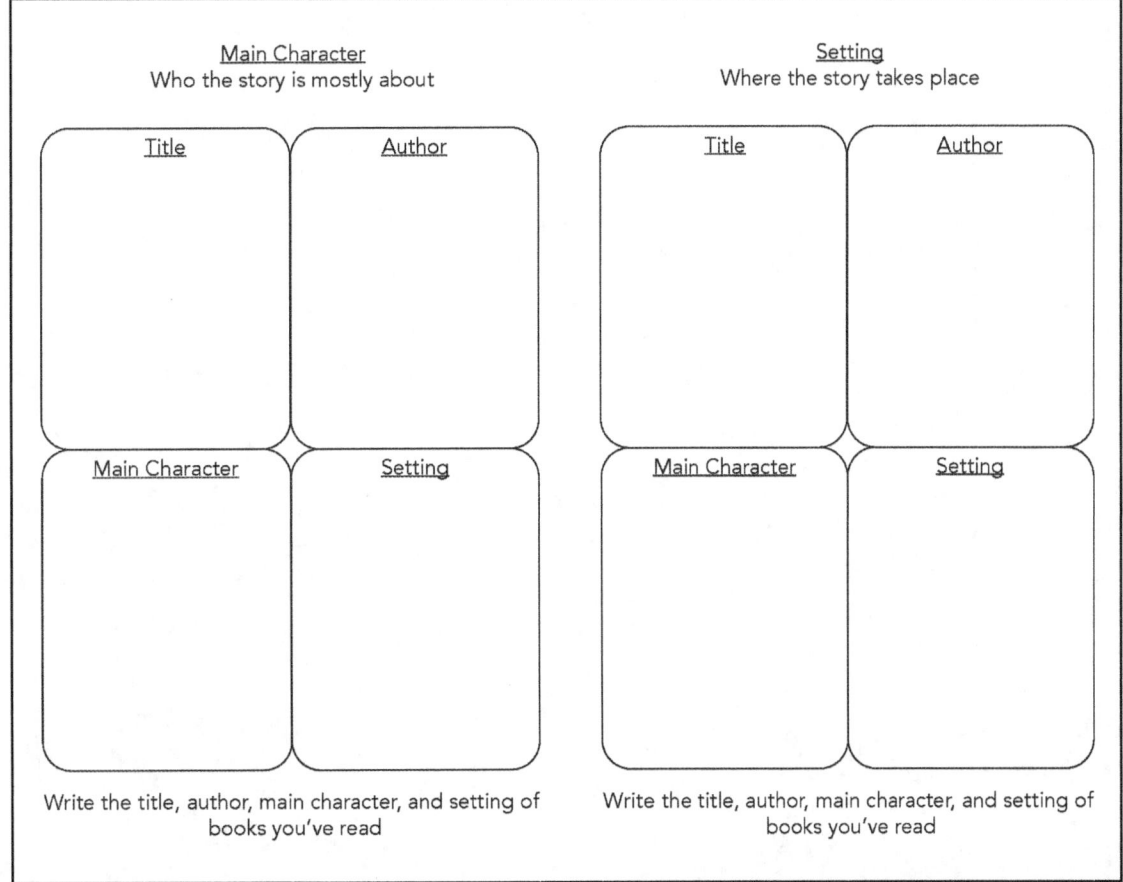

Main Character
Who the story is mostly about

Title

Author

Main Character

Setting

Write the title, author, main character, and setting of books you've read

Setting
Where the story takes place

Title

Author

Main Character

Setting

Write the title, author, main character, and setting of books you've read

Write and draw about an important event in your life

My Book of Important Events

By: _____

School: _____

Teacher: _____

Date: _____

Read two books.
Then draw and write three important events

Book 1 Title: _____

Book 2 Title: _____

Tell how you connect to the main character from a fiction book:

_____

_____

_____

_____

_____

My Book of Connections

By: _____

School: _____

Teacher: _____

Date: _____

Read two books and list the important facts or events you read about.
Then complete the sentence starters

_____
Non-Fiction Book Title

_____

_____

_____

My connection is...

_____

_____

_____

_____
Fiction Book Title

_____

_____

_____

This story reminds me of...

_____

_____

_____

Student booklets are available via the QR code at the end of the book

Think of two important people in your life.
In the diagram below, list how they are the same
and different.

Person 1

Same

Person 2

**My Book of Characters That
are the Same and Different**

By: _____

School: _____

Teacher: _____

Date: _____

Read two stories.
Then list how the main characters are the same and different in the diagram below.

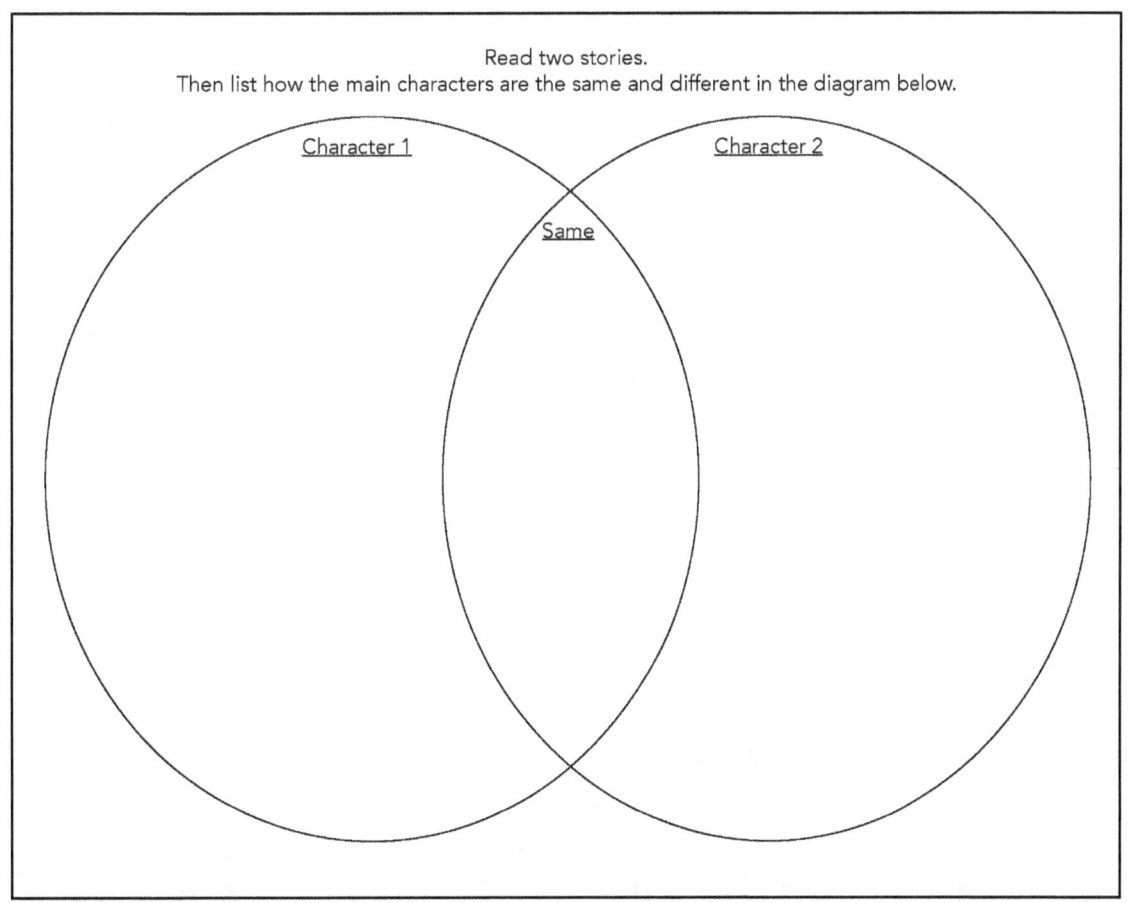

Character 1

Same

Character 2

Student booklets are available via the QR code at the end of the book

List facts about yourself:

My Book of _____
Facts (topic)

By: _____

School: _____

Teacher: _____

Date: _____

Read two books and list the important facts or events you read about.

Non-Fiction Book Title

Fiction Book Title

Student booklets are available via the QR code at the end of the book

Pretend you are writing a book about your favorite memory. Create a title, picture(s), and heading to help the reader predict what your book is about.

My Book of Predictions

By: _____

Title: _____

Picture(s):

School: _____

Teacher: _____

Heading: _____

Date: _____

Using a non-fiction book, find the following text features and make a prediction of what the book will be about.

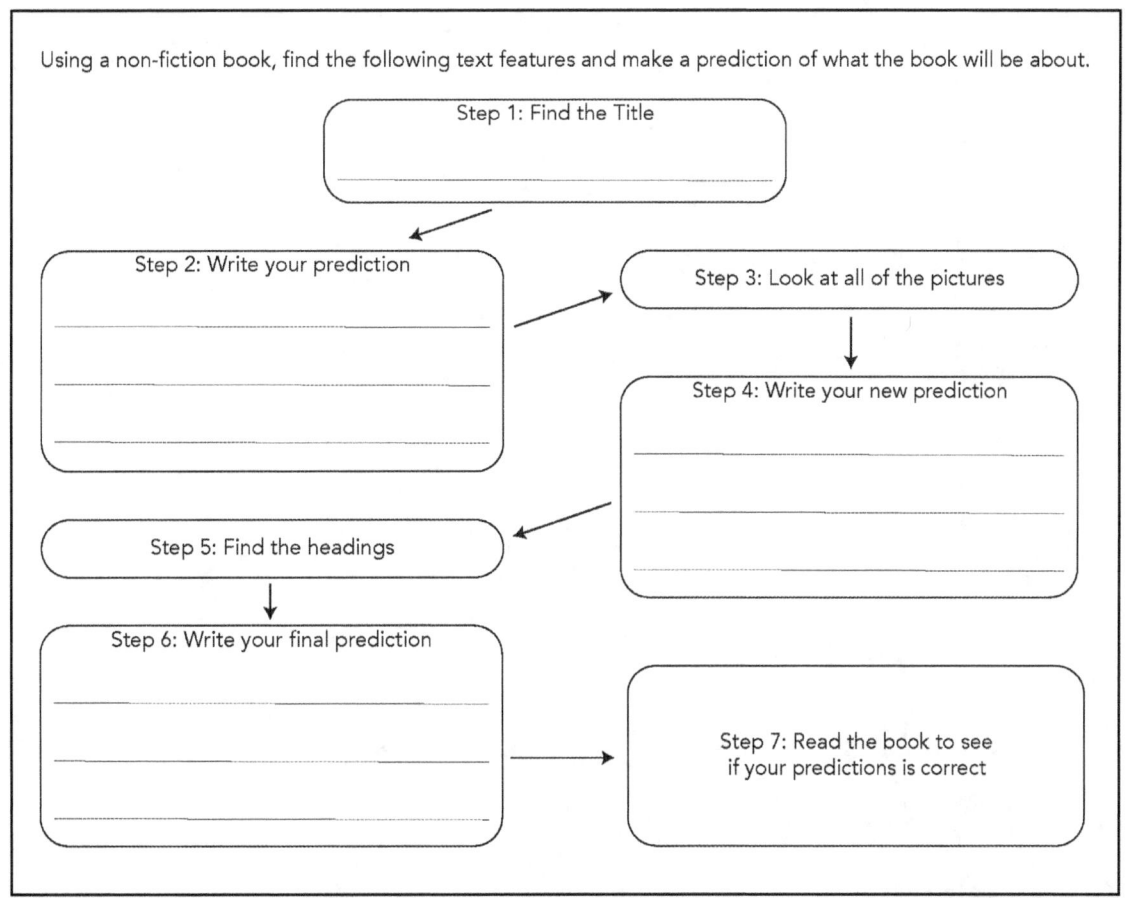

Step 1: Find the Title

Step 2: Write your prediction

Step 3: Look at all of the pictures

Step 4: Write your new prediction

Step 5: Find the headings

Step 6: Write your final prediction

Step 7: Read the book to see if your predictions is correct

CONTINUE CREATING LITERARY EXPERTS

BONUS BOOKLETS

A quick internet search for literary terms brings up hundreds of words. In addition, there are many topics to study as students gain more meaning from language and increase their writing skills.

Thus, the following blank pages are designed for students to write additional booklets about literary terms not included in *How to Create Language Experts with Literary Terms*. After selecting a new term, students select the format that best fits the task of writing about the literary term or concept.

There are times when children become so engrossed with a particular term that they want to make their booklet larger. These blank pages can also be used to add to existing booklets included in *How to Create Language Experts with Literary Terms*.

Student booklets are available via the QR code at the end of the book

My Book of _____

By: _____

_____

School: _____

Teacher: _____

Date: _____

_____
Title of Book 1

_____
Title of Book 2

Student booklets are available via the QR code at the end of the book

My art:

Student booklets are available via the QR code at the end of the book

Book 1 Title: _____   Book 2 Title: _____

Book Title

Book Title

Student booklets are available via the QR code at the end of the book

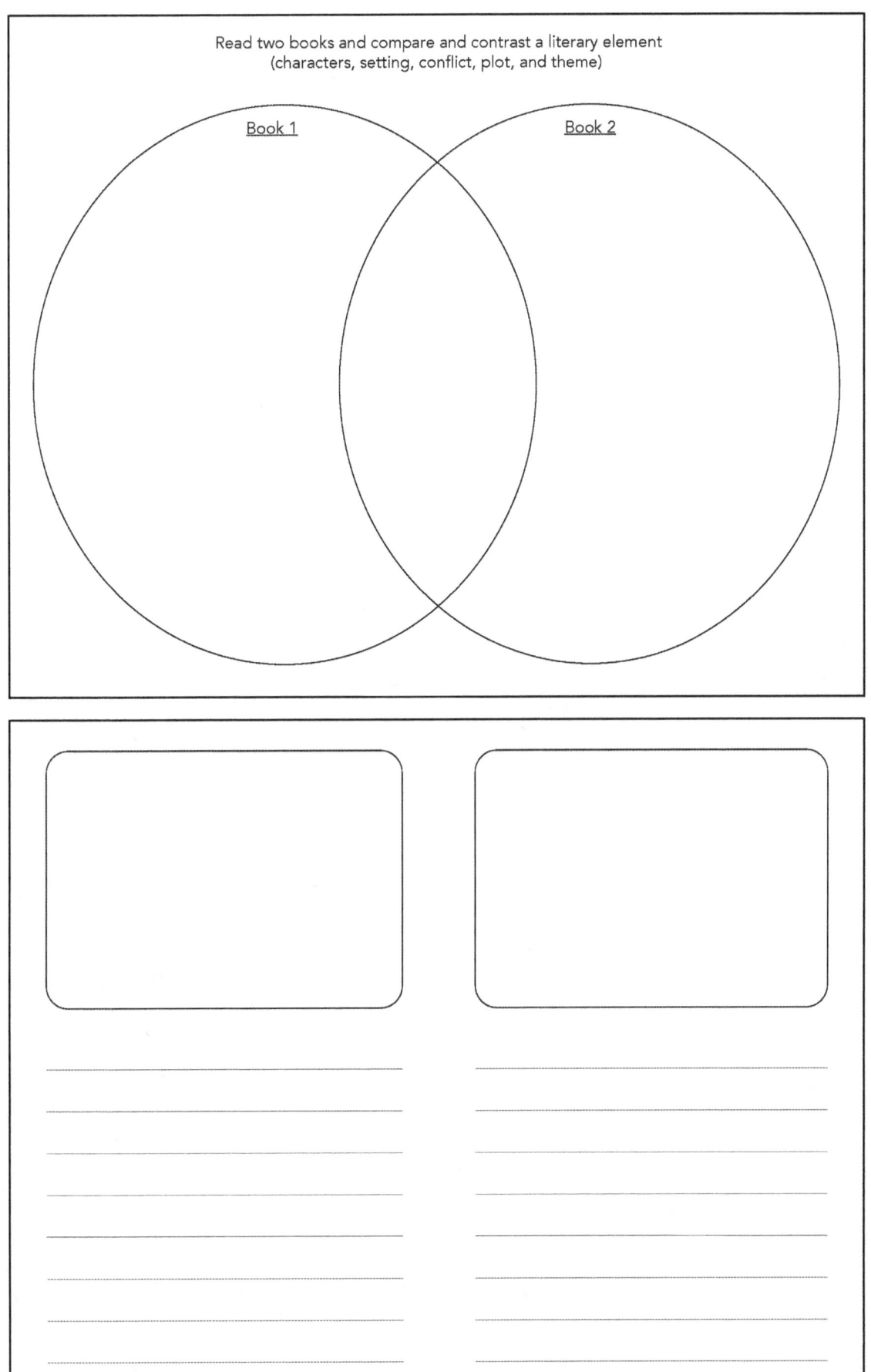

Read two books and compare and contrast a literary element
(characters, setting, conflict, plot, and theme)

Book 1

Book 2

Student booklets are available via the QR code at the end of the book

_____   _____
Book Title   Book Title

_____   _____
Title of Book One   Title of Book Two

Student booklets are available via the QR code at the end of the book

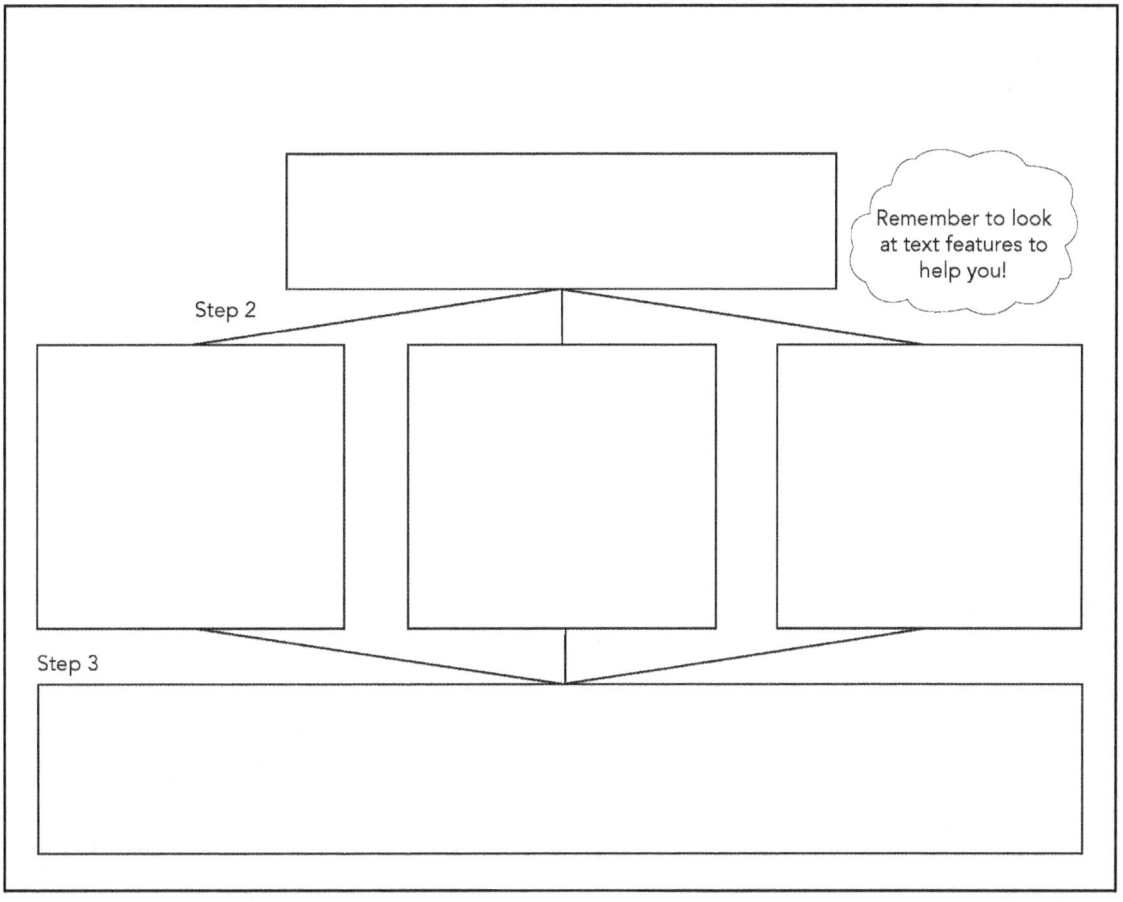

Step 2

Remember to look at text features to help you!

Step 3

Student booklets are available via the QR code at the end of the book

STUDENT BOOKLET DOWNLOAD

Purchasers of **How to Create Language Experts with Literary Terms** may use this QR code to download booklets from this book at no extra cost. This will ease the process of making copies for students and expand learning options. Both the print and digital download versions of this material are protected by copyright laws.

QR codes can be found in all LtoJ books, providing access to digital downloads of student worksheets.

ABOUT THE AUTHORS

Codi Hrouda grew up in the small town of Hubbard, Nebraska. After completing high school, Codi went on to pursue her degree in Elementary Education at Wayne State College, and graduated with a BA in Elementary Education in 2000.

Once graduated, Codi accepted her first job at Thurston Elementary School, in Thurston, Nebraska, as a fifth and sixth grade combination teacher. A year later, she and her husband moved to Columbus, Nebraska where she taught a year of first grade and then thirteen years of fourth grade at Centennial Elementary School. While teaching full-time in Columbus, she completed her master's degree in Curriculum and Instruction through Wayne State College. She graduated with her master's degree in May of 2006.

In 2014, Codi and her husband moved their family back to the area where she grew up to raise their three daughters. Codi accepted a fifth grade position at Dakota City Elementary in Dakota City, Nebraska where she continues to teach today. She just completed her twenty-second year of teaching in 2022. Codi spends her free time attending her daughters' activities, decorating, reading, and spending time with her family and friends.

Emma McInerney grew up in the small town of Elk Point, South Dakota. After completing high school, Emma went on to pursue a degree in healthcare at South Dakota State University (SDSU).

In 2015, she realized she was ready for a career change because her passion lies in education. She transferred to Dakota State University (DSU), earned a degree in Elementary Education, and graduated in 2019. Emma began her first job at Dakota City Elementary, in Dakota City, Nebraska, as a fifth grade teacher. While teaching full-time she completed her Masters degree in Curriculum and Instruction through Wayne State College, graduating in May of 2022. Emma concluded her third year of teaching in 2022, and she continues to teach alongside her co-author, Codi Hrouda.

Emma returned to her hometown of Elk Point after graduating, and spends her free time reading, gardening, and spending time with her boyfriend, family, and friends.

Dr. Lyle Lee Jenkins is an author, speaker, and recognized authority in improving educational outcomes. He believes that implementing a growth mindset and celebrating progress are the keys to helping students learn more and retain their enthusiasm for school.

His education experience, that spans over 50 years, ranges from working as a teacher, a principal, and a school superintendent in the California School System to being a University Professor. In 2003, Lyle Lee founded LtoJ, LLC hoping to impact and guide the way we approach education.

Lyle Lee Jenkins has authored six books showcasing continuous improvement in schools, including *How to Create a Perfect School*, *Optimize Your School*, *Permission to Forget*, *From Systems Thinking to Systemic Action*, *Improving Student Learning*, and *How to Create a Perfect Home School*. All literature offers powerful, practical suggestions for every aspect of education. The two most influential people supporting Dr. Jenkins's work are W. Edwards Deming and John Hattie.

Having spoken to educators all across the United States, Latin America, Europe, Australia, and Asia, Lyle Lee Jenkins is passionate about equipping the next generation with a true love of learning.

Dr. Lyle Lee Jenkins holds a Bachelor of Arts degree from Point Loma Nazarene University, a Masters of Education from San Jose State University and a Ph.D. from the Claremont Graduate University.

Lyle Lee Jenkins's website, www.LtoJ.net, is a great place to discover useful tools to guide your educational journey.

Do you have a great photo or video of your student using one of our products?

We would love the opportunity to share it on our website and social media channels!

Email us at info@ltoj.net

If you have a story to share, we would also like to hear from you. We feature student stories during presentations and on our social media accounts.

Our team loves sharing the joy of a child understanding new concepts. It allows our audience to experience firsthand the mission our team works towards every day; for students to maintain the same love of learning they brought to Kindergarten throughout all their years of schooling and into adulthood.

Thank you for being a loyal customer. We appreciate you!

The LtoJ Team

Follow us on Instagram, Facebook, TikTok and YouTube
@LtoJLLC